ENVIRONMENTAL FOOTPRINTS

How Big Is Your Clothing Footprint?

Paul Mason

Marshall Cavendish
Benchmark

New York

This edition first published in 2010 in the United States of America by Marshall Cavendish Benchmark.

Marshall Cavendish Benchmark
99 White Plains Road
Tarrytown, NY 10591
www.marshallcavendish.us

All Internet sites were available and accurate when sent to press.

First published in 2008 by
MACMILLAN EDUCATION AUSTRALIA PTY LTD
15–19 Claremont Street, South Yarra 3141

Visit our website at www.macmillan.com.au or go directly to www.macmillanlibrary.com.au

Associated companies and representatives throughout the world.

Copyright © Paul Mason 2008

Library of Congress Cataloging-in-Publication Data

Mason, Paul.
   How big is your clothing footprint? / by Paul Mason.
   p. cm. – (Environmental footprints)
   Includes index.
   ISBN 978-0-7614-4410-7
   1. Clothing and dress–Environmental aspects–Juvenile literature. 2. Clothing and dress–Environmental aspects–Case studies–Juvenile literature. I. Title.
   GT518.M338 2009
   391–dc22
                              2008048101

Edited by Anna Fern
Text and cover design by Cristina Neri, Canary Graphic Design
Page layout by Domenic Lauricella
Photo research by Legend Images
Illustrations by Nives Porcellato and Andrew Craig

Printed in the United States

Acknowledgments
The author and the publisher are grateful to the following for permission to reproduce copyright material:

Front cover photograph: Earth from space © Jan Rysavy/iStockphoto; colored footprint © Rich Harris/iStockphoto. Images repeated throughout title.

Photos courtesy of:
AAP Image/AFP/EPA, **11**; AAP Image/Photoalto, **29**; American Apparel, Inc, **13**; © Paha_l/Dreamstime.com, **7**; © Sebcz/Dreamstime.com, **21**; Gareth Cattermole/Getty Images, **12**; China Photos/Getty Images, **19**; Amanda Edwards/Getty Images for Chopard, **18**; Daniel Pepper/Getty Images, **9**; Tom Stoddart/Getty Images, **15**; Sylvain Grandadam/Image Bank/Getty Images, **20, 28**; Dana Edmunds/Taxi/Getty Images, **27**; © vera bogaerts/iStockphoto, **24**; © Graça Victoria/iStockphoto, **23**; Patagonia, **3** (top right), **16**; © Anyka/Shutterstock, **6**; © Galina Barskaya/Shutterstock, **30**; © Dewitt/Shutterstock, **10**; © Elena Elisseeva/Shutterstock, **8**; © N Joy Neish/Shutterstock, **17**; © Jennifer Nickert/Shutterstock, **22**; © Losevsky Pavel/Shutterstock, **5** (top); © Ilya Rabkin/Shutterstock, **26**.

While every care has been taken to trace and acknowledge copyright, the publisher tenders their apologies for any accidental infringement where copyright has proved untraceable. Where the attempt has been unsuccessful, the publisher welcomes information that would redress the situation.

Please note
At the time of printing, the Internet addresses appearing in this book were correct. Owing to the dynamic nature of the Internet, however, we cannot guarantee that all these addresses will remain correct.

Contents

Glossary Words

When a word is printed in **bold**, you can look up its meaning in the Glossary on page 31.

Environmental Footprints

This book is about the footprints people leave behind them. But these are special footprints. They are the footprints people leave on the **environment**.

Heavy Footprints

Some people leave heavy, long-lasting footprints. They do this by:

- acting in ways that harm the environment
- using up lots of **natural resources**, including water, land, and energy

It can be hundreds of years before the environment recovers from heavy footprints.

Light Footprints

Other people leave light, short-lived footprints. They do this by:

- behaving in ways that harm the environment as little as possible
- using the smallest amount of natural resources they can

The environment recovers from light footprints much more quickly.

As the world's population grows, more natural resources will be needed. It will be important not to waste resources if we are to leave light footprints.

The world's population is expected to continue growing in the future.

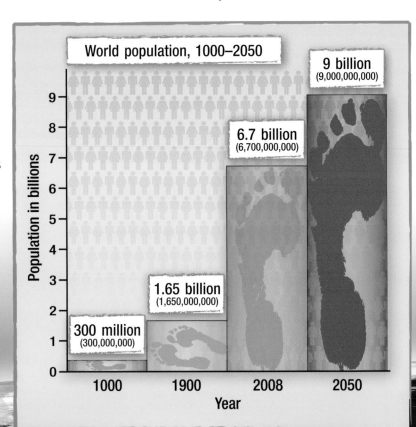

World population, 1000–2050

9 billion (9,000,000,000)

6.7 billion (6,700,000,000)

1.65 billion (1,650,000,000)

300 million (300,000,000)

Population in billions

Year

1000 1900 2008 2050

The journey of these clothes from cotton field to shop leaves a footprint on the environment.

What Makes Up a Clothing Footprint?

A clothing footprint is made up of the effects that the clothes people wear have on the environment. It includes every step in the life of the clothing, such as:

- the way crops are grown to make the cloth
- how the cloth is made
- how the clothes are **manufactured**
- the way clothes are transported
- how the clothes are **packaged** for sale
- the way the clothes are cleaned

All these things have an effect on the environment.
The bigger the effect, the heavier the footprint left behind.

What sort of clothing footsteps are you taking? Read on to find out!

The Clothing Industry

The clothing industry is made up of everything that puts clothes on people's backs. It includes growing fibers, weaving the fibers into cloth, manufacturing the clothing, and transporting the clothing to stores to be sold.

Cloth

Cloth can be made from **natural fibers** and **artificial fibers**. Natural fibers, such as cotton and wool, are still in their original form when they are made into clothes. The wool in a sweater, for example, started out as wool on a sheep.

Artificial fibers, such as polyester and nylon, are created from resources such as petroleum oil. Their natural form has been changed by humans, using chemicals and energy.

Mass Production

"Mass production" is when goods are made in large numbers. Mass production of clothes allows them to be produced quickly and at low cost. It usually happens in large workshops.

Nylon cloth for raincoats is made from petroleum oil.

These clothes have traveled around the world from their place of manufacture to the place where they will be sold.

An International Industry

The clothing industry spans the world. Clothing is usually made wherever it is cheapest, but often sold where people have the most money. This allows clothing companies to keep their costs low, but charge high prices. Some clothes travel a long way from where they were made to where they are worn.

Imagine the journey that could be taken by a cotton T-shirt.

1. The cotton is grown on a farm.
2. Then, it is made into cloth in a factory.
3. The cotton cloth is made into a T-shirt.
4. The T-shirt is then sold in a store.

Each of these steps happens in a different place. Sometimes, they even happen in different countries or continents.

Clothes are more affordable than ever before and many people have wardrobes full of clothes that are rarely worn.

Rethink!

Unwanted clothes can be given to thrift stores. Someone else gets to wear them, so the resources that went into making them are not wasted.

Benefits of the Clothing Industry

The modern clothing industry provides many benefits for shoppers.

⊕ There is a wide choice of comfortable fabrics that are easy to care for.

⊕ Mass production makes it possible to buy clothes for less money than ever before.

⊕ There is almost unlimited choice. Modern production and transportation allow stores to get new styles on their shelves in record time.

Most people in wealthy countries have far more clothes than people did fifty years ago.

Costs of the Clothing Industry

All of our new clothes come at a cost to the environment.

- Many of the **pesticides** used to grow most cotton crops can harm the environment. Pesticides are **poisonous** chemicals. They can pollute rivers and kill animals and plants, including those that do no harm to crops.

- The petroleum oil used to make artificial fibers is a precious natural resource. The world's petroleum is rapidly running out.

- The factories that make cloth and clothing use up precious water resources and create **pollution**.

- Transporting clothing also creates pollution.

- Washing or dry cleaning clothes after they have been worn uses up water and creates pollution.

About 20 percent of the world's pesticides are sprayed on cotton crops.

All these things harm the environment and make clothing footprints heavier.

Growing Fibers to Make Cloth

Much of the cloth we wear is made from natural fibers. Growing these fibers can damage the environment. This gives some clothes a heavy footprint.

Farming with Chemicals

Many cotton farmers grow their crops with the help of chemicals, especially **fertilizers** and pesticides. Cotton grown using these chemicals has a heavy footprint.

Fertilizers

Fertilizers are added to soil to make cotton plants grow bigger and faster. The fertilizers wash into rivers and lakes when it rains. There, they help **algae** and weeds to grow. The algae and weeds use up all the **oxygen** in the water, so there is none left for other creatures. The rivers and lakes slowly become clogged and lifeless.

This river has become clogged by algae because of fertilizer run-off from farms.

Rethink!

The fibers from a tough plant called hemp can be used as an alternative to cotton. Growing hemp uses far less water than growing cotton.

Taking water for irrigation caused the Aral Sea to dry up and shrink to half its former size.

Pesticides

Pesticides are used to stop insect pests from damaging crops. Unfortunately, the pesticides also kill insects that do useful jobs, such as helping plants to **reproduce**. The pesticides, which are poisonous, also get into rivers and lakes.

Water Use

Growing cotton uses large amounts of water. Cotton grows best in warm climates, where water is often in short supply. In some parts of the world, so much water has been used to **irrigate** cotton crops that the land has turned to **desert**.

Organic Cotton

Organic cotton is grown without using chemical fertilizers or pesticides. Some organic cotton farmers in India, for example, use a combination of chili, garlic, and soap to keep pests away. These farmers mainly use rainwater to water their crops. All this gives their organic cotton a much lighter footprint.

Hemp

Fiber from hemp plants can be made into a cloth similar to cotton. Hemp cloth is tough and long-lasting. Hemp can be grown without chemicals and uses much less water than cotton. This gives hemp a lighter footprint than cotton.

Recycling Fabric

Old clothes can sometimes be **recycled** and turned into new cloth. This is less harmful to the environment than making new cloth from scratch, so it has a lighter footprint.

This designer dress made from recycled fabrics has a light footprint.

Choosing to wear clothes made from organic cotton, hemp, or recycled fabric will give you a lighter clothing footprint.

Case Study
Scrap-heap Cotton

When cotton clothes are made, scraps of fabric end up on the factory floor. Usually this scrap-heap cotton is swept up and thrown out. This wastes the resources that were used to grow the cotton.

New cotton fabric can be made from these factory floor scraps. The scraps are combined with water, then manufactured into new cotton fabric. This is then used to make clothes.

Because they use a resource that would otherwise be thrown away, clothes made of scrap-heap cotton have a very light environmental footprint.

This hat was made using scrapheap cotton.

Artificial Fabrics

Artificial fabrics for clothes include polyester and nylon. Artificial fabrics are made using **nonrenewable resources**, usually petroleum oil. This gives them a heavier environmental footprint than fabrics made from **renewable resources**, such as wool or hemp.

Using Resources

Making fabric from petroleum oil uses up resources. The amount of oil left in the world is shrinking. Soon, the last of this resource may be used up.

The fabrics are made using high temperatures, up to 536 degrees Fahrenheit (280 degrees Celsius). The high temperatures are produced using electricity. This electricity usually comes from burning **fossil fuels**, such as coal. Burning fossil fuels to make electricity creates greenhouse gases, which are slowly causing the world's temperature to rise. This is called **global warming**.

Burning fossil fuels creates greenhouse gases, which are causing global warming.

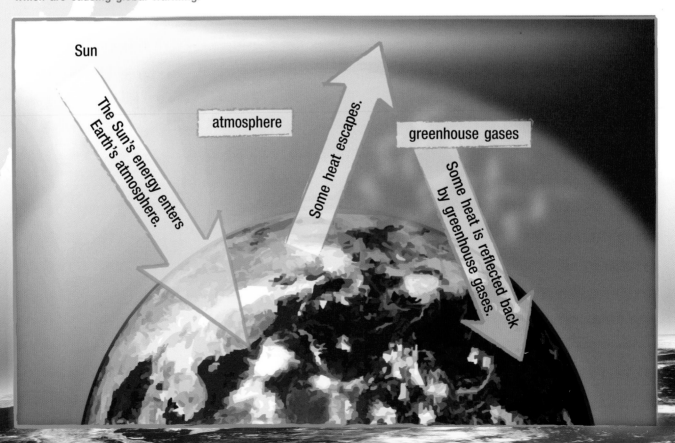

Sun

The Sun's energy enters Earth's atmosphere.

atmosphere

Some heat escapes.

greenhouse gases

Some heat is reflected back by greenhouse gases.

Dyeing

Artificial fabrics start life either white- or green-colored. Before being made into clothes, the material is usually dyed a new color. This process affects the environment in several ways.

The dyeing process uses electricity, which usually comes from burning fossil fuels.

The dyes are sometimes strong chemicals, which may be washed out of the factory and into the local water system. There, they pollute rivers and harm wildlife.

Finishing

Once artificial fabric is almost complete, it is "finished." Finishing usually involves spraying the fabric with some sort of chemical. These chemicals may escape into the environment, causing pollution.

These children in Kolkata, India, live near a waterway that has been polluted by a cloth-dyeing factory.

Rethink!

Repairing clothes makes them last longer. Repairing instead of replacing clothing means a lighter footprint on the environment.

Clothes from Plastic Bottles

Some artificial fabric has a lighter footprint because it is made from old plastic bottles. This is called PCR (post-consumer recycled) fabric.

Recycling Materials

Some clothing companies recycle artificial fabrics from their customers' old clothes. The customers return the clothes when they are worn out, and these are then **processed** and turned into new fabric. The new fabric can be used to make more clothes, which have a much lighter footprint than if they were made from new natural resources.

Reusing Materials

A few companies ask their customers to return parts of clothing that can be reused, such as brass buckles. Reusing old buckles on new clothes means that new brass buckles do not have to be made, so the new clothes have a lighter footprint.

PCR fabric, made of old plastic bottles, is often used in clothes for outdoor sports.

Choosing to wear fabrics made from renewable and recycled materials will give you a lighter clothing footprint.

Case Study
Artificial Versus Natural

For years, outdoor clothing manufacturers have used artificial fabrics for next-to-skin warmth. Manufacturing these fabrics, however, harms the land, rivers, and lakes, which are the very places that the people who buy the clothes enjoy!

Some manufacturers are now using a special fine merino wool as a natural alternative. Unlike artificial fabrics, the wool:

- comes from a renewable resource (the sheep can always grow more wool!)
- is biodegradable and will rot away without harming the environment

Merino wool is ideal for sports clothing and has a lighter footprint than artificial fibers.

New Zealand is one of the world's leading producers of fine merino wool for outdoor clothing.

Pollution from Making Clothes

Manufacturing clothes and transporting them to where they are sold releases pollution. The more harm this causes the environment, the heavier the footprint the clothes have.

Special Treatments

Special treatments or finishes are used to give clothes a particular look or feel. These include:

- washing out extra dye, which uses a lot of precious water
- using chemicals to make clothes look worn, which causes pollution
- treating wool with a powerful chemical called chlorine to make it feel softer, which causes pollution

All these things harm the environment, making the footprint of the clothes heavier.

Clothes that have been designed to look old do not last as long, and so have a heavier footprint.

Rethink!

Jeans that look broken in are actually a bit worn out and do not last as long! Jeans that look brand new last longer and are better for the environment.

This clothing factory in China is a long way from where the clothes will probably be sold.

Manufacturing Clothes

Most clothes are manufactured in factories, which need electricity for lighting and to run the machines. At the moment, most electricity comes from fossil fuels, which contribute to global warming.

Transportation Pollution

Transporting clothes from where they are made to where they are sold causes pollution. Clothes whose transportation causes a lot of pollution have a heavy footprint.

Many clothes are made far from where they will be sold. This means that clothes often travel long distances by boat. Once they arrive, the clothes are loaded onto trucks to be taken to stores for sale. Boats and trucks burn fossil fuels, causing pollution and contributing to global warming.

Eco-Balls

Eco-balls are a way of washing extra dye out of denim. They are like rubbery golf balls. When new jeans are washed using eco-balls, all the extra dye is washed out so that people can wear the jeans without dye rubbing off on them. No chemicals are used, so jeans washed with eco-balls have a lighter footprint.

Local Manufacture

Clothes that are manufactured near to where they are sold have a lighter footprint than clothes from far away. If the clothes are also made from local fabrics, they have an even lighter footprint. Shorter distances traveled between all the steps in making and selling clothes means less pollution caused by transportation.

Boots made and sold locally do not have to travel far, and so have a lighter footprint.

Choosing to wear clothes that have been made and transported in ways that cause less pollution will give you a lighter clothing footprint.

Case Study
Light-Footprint Jeans

Many people wear jeans more often than any other type of clothing. Jeans are probably the biggest single part of their clothing footprint. Here are some tips for finding jeans that have a light footprint:

- The jeans will be made of organic or recycled cotton.

- The cotton will be locally grown and the jeans locally made.

- The jeans will not be artificially worn out or bleached (bleaching weakens cotton), so the fabric will not wear out easily.

- The stitching and fabric will be as tough as possible, so the jeans will not need to be replaced for a long time.

Look for jeans made from organic cotton with extra-strong stitching.

Cleaning Clothes

Everybody's clothes get dirty and smelly. This means they need to be cleaned. Washing or dry cleaning clothes affects the environment and makes people's clothing footprints heavier.

Washing Clothes

Washing clothes in a washing machine affects the environment in three main ways. Each of these makes people's clothing footprints heavier.

Water Use

Washing machines use a lot of water. Each wash uses up to 22 gallons (100 liters). In many parts of the world, too much water is being used. Water supplies are getting smaller and smaller, so there is less to go around.

Rethink!

Washing clothes at 86 degrees Fahrenheit (30 degrees Celsius) uses up to 40 percent less energy than washing them at high temperatures.

Drying clothes outside instead of in a dryer saves electricity.

Foaming laundry detergent cleans clothes, but pollutes the environment.

Energy

Washing machines use electrical energy. Usually electricity is made by burning fossil fuels, which contributes to global warming.

Detergent Pollution

Washing machines use **detergent**, or soap, to clean clothes. Most detergents are made with petroleum-based chemicals. When water is emptied from the washing machine, these polluting chemicals are washed away into the **sewers**. From there, they reach rivers and the ocean. The chemicals do not biodegrade, or break down. Instead, they build up, affecting plants and animals for years to come.

Dry Cleaning

Dry cleaning clothes uses poisonous chemicals. Some experts say that these are bad for people's health. If the chemicals escape into the water system, they are very damaging to the environment.

Efficient Washing Machines

Efficient washing machines use less water and energy than normal. Some washing machines use only 9 gallons (40 liters) of water per load. Using one of these makes people's clothing footprint lighter.

Nonpolluting Detergents

Nonpolluting detergents biodegrade once they have been washed into the environment. They do not contain **petrochemicals**, bleach, perfumes, or other pollutants. Washing clothes with these affects the environment for only a short time.

Less Washing

Washing clothes less often makes people's clothing footprints lighter. Clothes need less washing if:

⊕ they are a color that does not show marks

⊕ the clothes fit loosely, so they get less sweaty

⊕ they are made of natural fabrics that let heat out and do not get as sweaty as artificial fabrics

In a hot climate, loose-fitting clothing does not absorb as much sweat so it needs less cleaning.

Choosing to wash your clothes in ways that minimize pollution, water use, and energy use will give you a lighter clothing footprint.

Case Study

How Full Is Your Washing Machine?

One way for people to reduce their clothes-washing footprint is to completely fill the washing machine. This means they use the machine less frequently. It also divides the environmental cost of washing between more items of clothing.

A full load of twenty items makes the most of the detergent, electricity, and water needed to run your washing machine.

One wash uses:
- 1 quantity of detergent
- 5 units of electricity
- 13 gallons (60 l) of water.

5 items

1 x T-shirt
1 x jeans
1 x underwear
2 x socks

20 items

5 x T-shirts
3 x jeans
8 x underwear
4 x socks

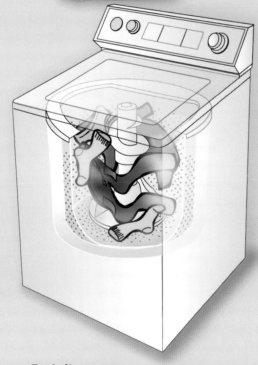

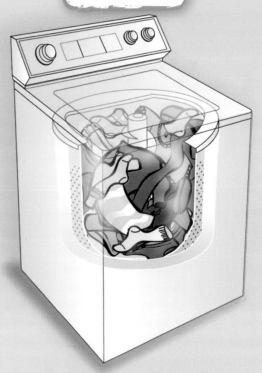

Each item uses:
- one-fifth of the detergent
- one unit of electricity
- 2.6 gallons (12 l) of water.

Each item uses:
- one-twentieth of the detergent
- one-quarter of a unit of electricity
- 0.7 gallons (3 l) of water.

Fashion and the Environment

The fashion industry introduces new styles several times a year. But there are alternatives to buying new clothes every season.

Secondhand Clothes

Secondhand clothes are a good way to get inexpensive, nearly new clothes. They have a light environmental footprint, because wearing secondhand clothes means not having to make new ones.

Refashioning Clothes

Refashioning clothes means adapting them so that they look different. This could involve taking up the hems of long pants to make shorts or re-stitching the seams on a T-shirt to change its shape. It can mean using fabric from old clothes to make completely new ones. Refashioning clothes has a far lighter footprint than buying new ones.

Shopping at secondhand vintage clothing stores is fashionable and has a light clothing footprint.

Choosing to wear secondhand or refashioned clothing will give you a lighter footprint.

Case Study
Wardrobe Refashion

Wardrobe Refashion is an online community of people who share ideas and techniques for making, altering, and mending clothes.

Rule number 1 is "No buying new!" Members promise not to purchase new manufactured items for two, four, or six months.

Instead they refashion pre-loved items for themselves with their own hands. They post on the website regularly to let each other know how their projects are going.

Originally set up in Australia, Wardrobe Refashion now has members in Japan, South America, the United Kingdom, and the United States.

Refashioning clothing is a fun, creative way to reduce your clothing footprint.

How Big Is Your Clothing Footprint?

The size of a person's clothing footprint depends on what their clothes are made of, where they come from, and how long they last. How big do you think your footprint is?

What Kind of Clothes Do You Wear?

Clothes with a light environmental footprint are made from cloth that:

⊕ does not harm the environment while it is being grown or made, such as organic, reused, or recycled cloth

⊕ lasts a long time, so that the clothes do not have to be replaced.

Light-footprint clothes also:

⊕ are not transported long distances before being sold

⊕ can be washed at low temperatures, to save energy

⊕ need to be cleaned less often than normal, saving water and stopping chemicals being released into the environment.

How big do you think your clothing footprint is?

These boots, made from local materials in a factory in Texas and sold nearby, have a light footprint.

Look through your clothes to check how heavy your footprint is.

Work Out Your Clothing Footprint!

Look through your clothes with a pad and pencil handy.
For each item of clothing, give yourself the following points:

- ⊕ **1 point** for anything worn more than once a week
- ⊕ **5 points** for anything more than 1 year old
- ⊕ **5 points** for anything you know was made within 100 miles (160 kilometers) from where you live.
- ⊕ **10 points** for anything made of hemp, organic cotton, or recycled fabric.

You have to take away some points, too! Take away:

- ⊕ **1 point** for anything not worn for a month or more
- ⊕ **5 points** for anything not worn for a year
- ⊕ **5 points** for anything less than 3 months old.

The bigger your score, the lighter your footprint!

Future Clothing Footprints

You can choose to take light footsteps or heavy footsteps. If people continue leaving heavy footprints, it could affect the environment for thousands of years to come.

What You Can Do

The Internet is a great way to find out more about what you can do to take lighter footsteps. Try visiting these websites:

⊕ **http://greenlivingideas.com/clothing-and-fashion/index.php**
There is lots of advice here on how to lighten your clothing footprint.

⊕ **http://nikkishell.typepad.com/wardroberefashion/**
This site is home to an international online community of people who make new, fashionable clothes out of old ones, instead of buying new clothes from stores.

Some of the search terms you might use to find interesting information about clothing and the environment include:
⊕ organic cotton
⊕ hemp
⊕ recycled cotton.

Why not try making some clothes from recycled fabric and yarn?

What will YOU do to change your clothing footprint in the future?

Glossary

algae
plantlike organisms that usually live in water, but do not have leaves, roots, flowers, or seeds

artificial fibers
fibers that do not come directly from nature, but instead are made by humans, often using petrochemicals

desert
area with very little water, where only certain plants and animals can live

detergent
cleaning material, usually a liquid or powder, that cleans away dirt and oil

efficient
working with the minimum amount of waste

environment
the natural world, including plants, animals, land, rivers, and seas

fertilizers
materials that help crops to grow; some fertilizers are natural, while others are artificially made using chemicals

fossil fuels
the remains of plants and animals from millions of years ago, which have been buried deep under Earth's surface and there turned into coal, oil, and gas

global warming
process by which Earth's average temperature is getting warmer

irrigate
supply water to a dry area to help crops grow

manufactured
made, or turned from raw materials into a product for people to buy and use

natural fibers
fiber from plants or animals, such as cotton or wool, which can be spun and woven into cloth

natural resources
natural substances, such as wood, metal, coal, or water, which can be used by humans

nonrenewable resources
resources that cannot be easily replaced, such as fossil fuels, which take millions of years to replace

oxygen
common gas that has no color or smell, which humans breathe and which can cause fires to burn and spread

packaged
wrapped up ready for people to buy in forms such as cardboard boxes, plastic bags, cans, or foam cartons

pesticides
poisonous chemicals used to kill pests, such as insects, fungi, and weeds, to prevent them from damaging crops

petrochemicals
chemicals made from petroleum oil or natural gas

poisonous
causes sickness or death to living things

pollution
damaging substances, especially chemicals or waste products, that harm the environment

processed
changed or prepared in a special way

recycled
used materials from an old, worn-out product to make a new product

renewable resources
resources that can be easily replaced

reproduce
make again

sewers
pipes and tunnels that carry away wastewater

Index

A

Aral Sea,   11
artificial fibers,   6, 9, 14–16

C

chemicals,   6, 9, 10, 15, 18, 20,
   23, 28
cloth,   6, 7
clothing footprint,   5, 21,
   28–29
clothing industry,   6–9
cotton,   6, 7, 11, 21
cotton farming,   9, 10–11

D

detergent,   23, 24, 25
dry cleaning,   9, 22, 23
dyeing clothes,   15

E

eco-balls,   20
electricity,   14, 15, 19, 23
environmental footprints,   4

F

fabric finishing,   15, 18, 20, 21
farming,   10–11, 12
fashion industry,   26
fertilizers,   10
fossil fuels,   14, 15, 19

G

global warming,   14
greenhouse gases,   14

H

hemp,   11, 12, 14, 29, 30

I

irrigation,   11

J

jeans,   18, 20, 21

L

local manufacturing,   20, 21,
   28

M

mass production,   6, 8, 19

N

natural fibers,   6, 10–12, 17, 24
natural resources,   4, 9
nonrenewable resources,   14
nylon,   6, 14

O

organic cotton,   12, 21, 29, 30

P

pesticides,   9, 10, 11
petrochemicals,   9, 14, 23, 24
petroleum oil,   9, 14, 23
pollution,   9, 10, 11, 15, 18–19,
   20, 23
polyester,   6, 14
population growth,   4
post-consumer recycled (PCR)
   fabric,   16

R

recycled cloth,   12, 13, 16, 28
recycled cotton,   13, 30
refashioning clothing,   26, 27
renewable resources,   14, 17
repairing clothing,   14, 27
reusing clothing,   8, 16, 26, 30
rivers,   10, 11, 15, 23

S

scrap-heap cotton,   13
secondhand clothes,   8, 26

T

thrift stores,   8
transportation,   5, 8, 9, 19, 20,
   28

W

Wardrobe Refashion,   27, 30
washing clothes,   9, 22–25, 28
water use,   9, 11, 12, 18, 22, 23,
   24, 25
wool,   6, 14, 17, 18